Merry Christmas!

It's a Great Day To...
Gather Around a Table

Mary Yana Burau

Mary Yana Burau ♡

Some of the many ways my mom has shown love for me and my family were by creating memorable experiences together and taking the time to instill family and Christian values. This often started around a dinner table. After long days of school and sports, we could always count on having dinner together to hear about each other's days and discuss the trials of life as a family.

After leaving home for college, a few of the values and traditions continued as a shared time with friends, while others have reappeared now that I married Amanda. The time together with family, celebrating the birthday parties, sharing good meals, and other "It's a Great Day To" moments have been enjoyed by our friends and us. We continue to relish those times together with each passing year. Looking back on my upbringing, I am thankful for my family and particularly my mom for creating and establishing these traditions and good times.

Dr. Alexander Burau

Mary Yana and I have been together for 34 years. When you know someone for that long, you learn what drives them. She has been eager to be an author and write about her passion for most of those 34 years. Finally, with all her life experience, it's happening. The passion is there. She just needed a little "nudge" to move forward. It has been my pleasure as her husband and closest confidant to give her that "encouragement" to write her book.

Dr. Bradley A. Burau

I grew up in the "It's a Great Day To..." world, before the book and the blog had an official name. They've been a dream of my mom for years but didn't have a title. The food, the table, the organization, and the mindset were embedded into her parenting and were doctrine in our home.

In our home, our best education came from the dinner table. My parents prioritized time as a family a few times a week to sit and discuss one another's day. This simple act shaped our thinking, decision-making, and relationships. It helped us find the positive in our day-to-day routines, and we learned to grow even on the tough days. My mom created the environment for this through a meal at home and a set table.

In a world where we are so interconnected yet so distanced by technology, she inspires us to make the simple tasks special and take more time not only to be together but to be present.

Sasha Burau Meyer, CEO Drs. Burau & Downtown Dental

Having grown up in the house of "It's a Great Day To...," I was taught lessons that prepared me for adulthood. This book not only holds great tips for preparing the best home-cooked meals or sprucing up the house for entertaining guests, it also holds tips and tricks to living your best life that all families should listen to. In a time where family values are lacking, this book is a necessity in every household.

Zachary Burau, FLYLINE Founder & CTO

Make no mistake. This gorgeous book is not really about food, cooking, or entertaining. Inside, you will find recipes for living a genuinely happy life—starting with the items on our own daily "to do" lists. Mary Yana inspires us to savor the joyful opportunities of each day.

With a message that couldn't be timelier, Mary Yana illustrates how to take unapologetic pleasure in spending time at home with family and friends, and putting faith and the "Big Picture" first in daily life. (And yes, eating well *is* a part of living well—so be prepared to treasure her recipes too.)

Mary Yana's signature phrase "It's a Great Day to..." reminds us to pause and make the daily decision to transform each day into a great day. Mary Yana has made my life happier and better. Her friendship and perspective are gifts that have inspired me for decades. Now, with "It's a Great Day to Gather Around a Table," this gift is yours too.

Denise (Sheehan) Couling
August 2, 2020

Acknowledgment

When you start a project like this, you realize that no one can do this by themselves. It takes a TEAM. Like Bo Schembechler, the famed University of Michigan football coach, said in his famous locker room speech, "The TEAM, the TEAM, the TEAM." It's all about a TEAM. Here are mine.

1. Michelle Prince, the book publisher who saw the vision.
2. Ana, the project coordinator who brought the design team and copy editors together and listened to my tech inadequacies, compensating where I lacked.
3. Jamie O'Brien, who set up my media and website and taught me so much.
4. The Close Friends who cheered me on.
5. Austin R. Speer, who took gorgeous cover photos making us all look quite good.
6. Denise Couling, a childhood friend who saw what I did not see and encouraged me to make this happen.
7. My Mother-in-law and Father-in-law who cheered us on.
8. My Brother, who always is there for our Family.
9. My Parents, who instilled in me a strong "Don't give up" work ethic.
10. Our kids, Sasha, Dan, Zach, Alex, and Amanda, who are all faithful, kind, hardworking, smart, and industrious. Seeing them doing well makes me proud, and I appreciate all of their encouragement and feedback.
11. My Husband, who is always honest, generous, faithful, and encourages me to see my dream through.
12. Our Lord and Savior, Jesus Christ, through whom all things are possible.

It's a Great Day To...
Gather Around a Table

It is an interesting time we are living in now in 2020. Technological advances have made it possible for us to gain knowledge at the tip of our fingers via a computer, iPad, or smartphone. We can pick up a phone and be in touch with anyone in the world, and we shop, pay for, and have delivered anything we want in a matter of a few hours or overnight. If we decide last minute we want or need to be across the country or across the pond, we can search, book, and pay for a flight on our phones and be on our way within a short period of time. A New York to London flight can be made in under six hours. For most of us, the economy was pretty good until just a few shorts months ago when everything came to a screeching halt in late March. However, technology made it possible for kiddos to connect with teachers, and Families could connect with one another during quarantine despite the precautions necessary to ensure everyone's safety during the pandemic.

So why do so many people feel lonely, disconnected, and unhappy? Well, I have a few theories based on my fifty-seven years of life experience as an educator, wife, and mother of three kind, bright, and industrious adult children. For one, participation in organized religion is down in the U.S. (2019 Gallup Poll-70% of Americans in 1999 participated in organized religion while half of Americans participate unorganized religion as of 2019) and it is down in Europe as well. Today, the beautiful chapels and cathedrals of Europe are less occupied for religious purposes and more as museums. Religion brings people together, gives us hope, and helps us feel our purpose in the world. Secondly, extended Families live further apart than they used to. It is rare that extended Families gather for Sunday dinners, Family birthday parties, or holidays. Grandmothers used to be babysitters. Many grandmothers now work or live in another state or town. Careers and new and better opportunities cause Families to move away, and unless an effort is made by all parties, relationships can be strained, distant, or non-existent. People get busy and into their careers or new communities. Time goes by, and relationships can become weak. It's not meant to, but life gets busy.

Lastly, and most obvious to me, the thing that could make closer communication possible, can drive us apart ... THE PHONE! Well, not necessarily the phone itself, but what it allows us to do. It is our link to the world, our way to see what everyone else is doing, what is happening, and see who is communicating with us. It's a window to see all things shiny and available to us, which can be a good thing but can also be distracting when we are trying to have a conversation, a quiet car ride, or dinner with a Friend, a spouse or as a Family. How many times have you been out to dinner and observed a couple or Family with their phones out? They are more engaged with the phone than with the person or people around the table. It is sad. Very sad.

You may notice that I often capitalize Family. I do that for a reason. You see the Family is the strongest bond in society. "Blood IS thicker than water." Statistics prove that if one grows up in a Family with strong bonds, there is a good chance a child will grow up to be a happy and well-adjusted adult. I lived in an all-female dorm at the University of Michigan called the Martha Cook Building (MCB). It was built, in 1912, by William Cook, a U of M alumnus and very successful New York attorney. He named the dorm in honor of his mother. There is an inscription on the fireplace mantel in the dining room that has stuck with me all these years as a wife, mother, and teacher, and I have a needle-point version in our own kitchen, "HOME, the Nation's Safety." In addition to favorite Bible verses, this short phrase has helped guide me when making important decisions.

You see, if HOME is a safe and comfortable place, our Nation is in good shape, and we are strong. We all know the sad effects of the opposite. We can see it every day in the news, especially these days. So, whether you are single, a newly married couple, an established Family, an empty nester, a grandparent, or one who is starting a new chapter in your life, flip through this book and see how you can bring the people who gather around your table closer. Who knows what may happen? It's a Great Day.

About
Mary Yana Burau

Mary Yana was born in Flint, Michigan. Her dad immigrated from Bouf, Macedonia, and her mom came to Flint from Monroe, North Carolina. She has one younger brother, John Todorovsky, who followed her father's footsteps and went into the restaurant business. She grew up in Grand Blanc, Michigan, graduating from Grand Blanc High School. Later on, she attended and graduated from the University of Michigan, School of Education, in Ann Arbor. While at the university, she had the opportunity to live in the historical, beautifully decorated, all-female dorm, the Martha Cook Building, where sit-down dinners with waitresses occurred four days a week and tea was served on Friday afternoons. Living in the dorm and having close Friendships with her five Martha Buddies left an impact on her life that has long stayed with her. In fact, the inscription on the fireplace mantel in the MCB dining hall, "HOME, the Nation's Safety," along with her favorite Bible passages, has been a phrase that has guided her in teaching and raising her

Family.Mary Yana began her teaching career working in the Flint Community Schools, and then went on to teach parenting, home economics, and cooking classes. She and her husband Brad, a dentist, have raised three children. Sasha (and Dr. Dan Meyer) are parents to Stella, and Dr. Alex (and Amanda Robinson) Burau married in 2019. They all reside in Grand Blanc and work in the Family dental offices. Youngest son, Zach, is the founder of FlyLine, based in Dallas, Texas. In addition to cooking and writing, Mary Yana enjoys traveling, dance, and teaching Pilates at her local fitness gym, Ascension Genesys Health Club.

For more information and reading, check out Mary Yana's blog and recipes on Itsagreatdayto.com.

Contents

Chapter 1
It's a Great Day To...
Start with a Table

I remember shopping for our first kitchen table when we were engaged. As we shopped, I pictured in my mind Thanksgiving dinners, breakfast before school, Family birthday parties, late-night homework sessions, dinner parties with Friends, pretty dinner plates, platters, flatware, glasses, table linens, flowers, and candles. All of these visions danced in my head as we traveled from store to store, looking for the "perfect table" for us. Setting up one's adult life, a new marriage, or a new chapter involves some sort of setting up a kitchen, and just as the kitchen is the heart of the home, the table is the center of the kitchen.

In looking for a table, one needs to determine a budget, a size and shape, the color, and a style. When beginning a search, look for inspiration. Thirty-three years ago when we were looking, I cut photos from magazines and took photos of tables I saw. Favorite movie sets were also a form of inspiration. One of my favorite sources for inspiration was books from the library, and of those books, Laura Ashley design books were where most of my inspiration came from. Laura Ashley is a traditional British housewares and clothing design company founded in 1953 by Bernard and Laura Ashley. Having spent a semester in London and traveling through Great Britain on a few occasions, this style of home and design was of interest to me and was something I hoped to incorporate into a home someday. That experience remains in my heart all these years later, and I think will continue to, most likely because it brings to mind a very happy and informative time in my life.

Alex & Amanda's (our son and daughter-in-law) IKEA kitchen table beautifully set for a Mother's Day Brunch.

Pay attention to clues like that as you look into your own life for inspiration. I liked the very comfortable way the British decorated, with a bit of this and that, from here and there. But the constant variable seemed to be the adorable fabric and patterns that they put together, from a small floral chair cushion to a striped table cloth, to a busy and colorful English countryside of dishes that may or may not match. I loved that look and the way it made me feel when we stayed at a B&B (the pre-cursor to the current Airbnb) while traveling.

My husband grew up in a very traditional home. His mother has a fantastic eye for classic and traditional pieces. They have always lived in a very beautiful, clean, and organized home. She, too, shared my style of comfortable classic British design. This made shopping for a kitchen table and more furniture later on

A nice drop leaf table from a re-sale shop in Petoskey, Michigan, that makes a lovely round table in our sunroom.

much easier than it could have been because Brad, having grown up in a beautiful home, valued it for us as we began to merge our lives together as a young couple. We ended up with a classic round dark oak pedestal table from a local furniture store with a leaf and four chairs. We were quite proud of our first official purchase, getting what we considered a good price. We accepted delivery a few days before our wedding when we got possession of our first apartment together. We were happy to begin putting our "nest" together. We felt the most important purchase had been made. After all, everyone needs to eat and must have a place to do so.

The traditional Ethan Allen Farm House Table you will see in our kitchen throughout the book with a bench, chairs and cute printed fabric cushions. Check out Target, Walmart and IKEA for inexpensive cushions to go with your decor.

In looking for a table today, there are so many ways to be inspired for ideas, and so many places to shop. One can spend a small fortune to get the perfect table for their needs. Inspiration can now come from Pinterest, internet searches, virtual home internet sites, design websites, and online catalogues from one's favorite stores. Pottery Barn, Ballard Designs, Ethan Allen, the possibilities are endless and all without leaving one's couch.

Do your homework. Determine your budget and be honest. Ask what your needs are. If there is just one of you or if you are a young couple, do you really need to get the expensive large table to grow into? If you are blending two families then yes, you would need a larger table. Know your needs now and for the next couple of years. With Facebook Marketplace, it is very easy to buy and sell used furniture, but don't over spend for something and expect to get it back in a couple of years if your needs change. IKEA, the large Swedish furniture home design company, offers inexpensive furniture that has some appealing styles. The negative is that you pick it up and put it together yourself. That is why the price is so low. You can pay for delivery and assembly. For some, this is a good way to go. You need to assess your needs. Make sure you know the size you need that fits into your space. Measure and measure again. I used to shape newspaper in the size of furniture, whether it was a kitchen table, chair, or couch, to visualize the space. That worked for me to see the layout and how much space there was for everything in a room.

Decide on a color or wood finish for the table. One can mix finishes and colors. Do you like side chairs, or would a bench be more appropriate? Chairs with arms or no? I have seen very cute booths as well.

A square table from IKEA that folds out into a larger rectangular table, is a good option for a single, sans children or empty nest kitchen. Nicely set for dinner with another couple.

You can buy something used or unfinished and paint it yourself or have it painted by a handy person. Do your math, add up costs, and get any estimates in writing. Make sure you have the correct color in mind.

In addition to the table, there are dishes, flatware, linens, and chair pads that are needed, and these add to making an ordinary table your own. None of these need to be big ticket items, but when you add it all up, you can go overboard. So spend wisely. One does not need to spend too much on any of these. If you are getting married, you will probably do a bridal registry, but be sensible. Do not expect your guests to buy you something you wouldn't be comfortable buying for yourself or anyone else. If you break a dish, is it too expensive for you to replace? If the answer is yes, don't register for it. Use common sense.

If you are not getting married, go through what you have, and if you need a few new dishes to mix in, buy some to complement what you have. If you have a solid color, pick up a few in a print or pattern to mix in.

Amanda, our daughter-in-law, constructed this table for the dining room in their new home. The chairs were a gift from a dear friend of ours, which I passed onto Amanda and Alex.

If you have print dishes, a solid in a complementary color or solid white looks nice. If your dishes are fine, pick up some pretty placemats or a nice tablecloth. Again, you don't need to spend a lot to make a table look inviting. Good sources for pretty tablecloths, placemats, and napkins are the clearance sections at Williams-Sonoma, Sur La Table, Target, IKEA, Crate and Barrel, TJMaxx, and Home Goods. Be creative, and DO NOT OVERSPEND because you don't need to.

Next, candles, flowers, and vases help set the stage to make your table a place you want to gather at the end of the day with the person or people you love and look forward to being with. If you are solo, make plans to invite Family and/or Friends over. If it's not your thing, start small with a happy hour or tea, which we will discuss in a future chapter. And don't think you have to make everything. People love bringing something to contribute and to show their appreciation to the hostess for planning the gathering. I know a widowed lady in Florida who frequently has dinner parties. She likes being invited places with her couple friends and reciprocates, showing her appreciation for being included. Consequently, she always has something to do and friends to make plans with. One has to make an effort if they want to be included. Flowers picked up from the grocery store are easy, and I tend to select the varieties that last the longest, like daisies and alstroemeria. Place them in a vase that you have on hand or a large Mason jar. Once you have placed them in the vessel, make sure you can see the person across the table from you if you are using them for a dinner setting. Candles again, low in height. Inexpensive tea lights purchased from the Dollar Store or Walmart, placed in jam jars are nice, small, and add a little ambiance.

When we could not find the correct-sized dining room table to fit where we wanted to use it, we decided to design one to be made by the Amish Family who made our kitchen cabinets.

When setting the table, remember that the fork goes on the left side of the plate, on top or next to the napkin. An easy way to remember which side to put the fork is that the words *fork* and *left* both contain four letters. On the right of the plate is the *spoon* and *knife* which both have five letters as does the word *right*. I do not get credit for this way of remembering, but my college roommate Virginia does. She shared with me that when she attended the funeral of a ninety-something year old lady, her grandchildren eulogized her by relating the fond memories they had of their grandmother who taught them this way to remember setting the table. Love that she took the time to teach them a clever way to remember this skill and leave happy memories of their grandmother for a lifetime to remember and a story to pass on to their children.

You now have the knowledge to create the setting for a meal that will bring you together with those you care for. We will cover what to serve in the following chapter. With a few additional notes, we wrap this one up.

1. I recommend no technology at the table. Focus on those sitting around the table with you. When someone gets their phone out at a meal, they are sending the message that the person on the other end of the phone is more important than those present, unless there is an extenuating circumstance. If there are children at the table, they will model behavior. If you're out to dinner, it can be disruptive to those at a neighboring table. It's just NOT necessary unless there's an absolute emergency, and there are those situations at times.

2. Start small with one meal and see how that goes. We will check out a variety of meal options to choose from, coming up.

3. Give thanks for the meal and the hands who prepared it. Begin with a simple known prayer or one where everyone goes around the table giving thanks for their special blessing(s).

4. Everyone can help with clean up, so the host/hostess does not feel overwhelmed or is up late cleaning, long after guests have departed.

5. It's okay to ask for someone to help or bring something, and likewise, it is okay to make it all if one has a vision and prefers to do that. It is completely up to the one hosting.

Chapter 2
It's a Great Day To...
Start with a Dinner

So now that the stage is set, it's time to think about a meal to be enjoyed. I like starting with a dinner on a day when everyone will be around to enjoy it. For us, that would be a Sunday; however, any day when you can gather your people is a Great Day. I have a few different meal options to choose from depending on your available time, your schedule, or your experience in the kitchen. "Choose wisely," as Yoda from Star Wars says. We want this to be fun and successful, so don't get in over your head and become discouraged. Remember, "If Mama (or Daddy, or whoever is preparing) ain't happy, ain't nobody happy."

You set the mood, and everyone else will pick up on this. Select something that sounds good to you, keeping in mind everybody's dietary restrictions and likes/dislikes. If you have children, encourage them to eat what you are eating for a couple of reasons. One, make it easy on you. You are NOT a short order cook, and you shouldn't be expected to be. It is good for children to try new things early in life, so teach them how to keep an open mind when trying new foods. When they don't like something after trying it, teach them to be polite. If they don't like something, that's okay, but encourage them to try new things because they may just like it.

Once the menu has been selected and shopping done, get all the items out. Everyone has their own philosophy about food planning and prep. I like to make a large recipe, like double it, and plan on left-overs. Freeze in applicable portion size for your situation or plan on taking a nice dinner to someone who could use a little pick me up or "just because." As I chop, slice, and measure, I like to clean up as I go so there aren't too many items out and there is less mess at the end. But that is a personal preference. I have Friends who like to do the entire clean up at the end. Decide what your style is and make it part of your routine. If you have kiddos or a co-pilot, get them in on the action, put on some of your fav music, and get going. There are times, however, when I enjoy cooking solo as a way to wind down. Like some people go to yoga to chill and slow down, cooking and being in the kitchen can do that for me. It's all about finding your comfort zone. I feel the same way about cleaning up. If there is a big group, it does help to get every-one to pitch in because it goes quicker, of course, and it can be social as well. Likewise, cleaning up solo can be relaxing too. The process can be just as enjoyable as the meal.

I like a beverage to enjoy while prepping. For me, that would be a fruit-flavored soda water or a fav cider on a special occasion. I like a cute apron that fits the vibe of the day, season, or meal. My dad always wore a white apron with the sash wrapped around him twice and tied in front. I find myself doing that. I look for aprons on sale at Williams-Sonoma, Sur la Table, and Target, and I keep them in a kitchen drawer so they are easily accessible with one kept handy on a hook next to the oven. When I put my apron on, "It's Show Time," "The work day is done," Whatever your phrase, it's time to relax and call it a day from the outside world. It's time to enjoy your people.

Next, think about setting the table. Enlist someone to help, or do it yourself. When the kids were little, I would have them make the table look pretty, and I do the same with the kiddos when I teach a kids' class. They love selecting cloths, placemats, napkins, and dishes. If you are on the lookout for good sales in your colors, you can accumulate quite a collection to choose from. If it's just the two of us or we are having guests, I plan in advance what the table will look like.

Flowers and simple non-scented candles are nice (one would not want the heavy scent of a candle to take away from the aroma of a lovely home cooked meal). On hand, I keep a large bag of tea light candles (extremely inexpensive) in the kitchen. I add one of these little candles to a small Mason jar or an empty, clean jam jar. All table candles and flowers are kept low so that they can be enjoyed and everyone can see who they are sitting across from. I also use these containers for flowers as well. You can pick up a bunch of inexpensive flowers at the grocery store, and when divided into these small containers, they can be used not only for the table but on a bedside table to enjoy when waking up or in a guest bathroom.

I think you get the idea. Make the table look special. If you are going to the effort to make a dinner, let the table reflect it. I like cloth napkins because they can be washed and used again. I like the color/print they add to a table, but paper napkins are nice also. It is really just a preference.

After enjoying your dinner, decide how you will store leftovers. It depends on how you plan to use your leftovers. If they are to be enjoyed in the next 24-48 hours, store in airtight containers in the fridge. If freezing, freeze immediately (after cooling, of course) in appropriate freezer bags or containers. I store Bolognese sauce in one portion size freezer bags so that they can be taken out for a meal when one of us is home alone. If taking to a Friend/Family member, I usually take in freezer bags or Glad storage containers, not expecting to have returned. I tell the person that so that there is no pressure to return the container. Make it easy, and you will do it more often. It's a nice thing to do.

With all that said, decide on a meal and get going. Once you see how enjoyable it is to sit down with no technology—just some nice music in the background, nice conversation, your favorite beverage, all savored with people you love—you WILL find a few times each week to "Gather Around a Table."

Rotisserie Chicken Dinner

Rotisserie Chicken picked up on the way home after a busy day, served on a pretty glass table, with wild rice green beans, salad and Sangria (chapter 7) to drink. Why not?

4-5 SERVINGS

So this would be your easiest "go-to" meal. It's a busy afternoon. You don't have time to make a detailed dinner. You didn't have time to get something going in a slow cooker this morning, and you would just rather not run through the drive-through. You need to make a quick trip to the grocery store, collect an already cooked rotisserie chicken from the deli (you may want to call ahead to make sure they still have some), and pick up some fresh or frozen vegetables. (Our favorites are green beans and broccoli, but you choose yours.) Also, pick up brown rice (either actual brown rice or a boxed brown rice mix), some fresh parsley, and your favorite ice cream or ice cream bars for dessert. That's it, and here's how to put it all together.

1 Rotisserie Chicken

1 French baguette from the bakery freezer section or unbaked in the bakery (Ask where to find them if you don't see them.)

1 head of broccoli, or a package of frozen green beans, or a handful of fresh green beans per person

1 cup of brown rice

2 cups of water

¼ teaspoon sea salt

1 tablespoon butter

½ bunch of parsley washed, stems cut off, and coarsely chopped tops (You'll buy a full bunch. Use half and have the other half for another meal. Rinse when you return home, store in a tall glass of water, and place in the fridge.)

1. When you get home, get the rice going as directed on the package/box. Bringing your water to a boil, add the salt, butter, and rice. Turn down low and simmer until done, approximately 30 minutes. Watch it so as not to burn or boil over. Turn off and remove pan from stove, and pour rice into a bowl to slightly cool.

2. Check baguette package for heating instructions and preheat oven. Place baguette directly onto rack in the oven and set timer.

3. While the rice cooks, set your table and cut your rotisserie chicken into serving pieces. Divide onto plates or place on a serving plate (depending on your style of serving dinner – either Family Style or preparing each person's plate for them, which is best when you have children. Steam your broccoli/green beans after washing and cutting into florets/ trimming beans. In a stockpot lined with a steamer basket, steam for about 5 minutes or until your desired doneness is reached. If using frozen veggies, prepare as directed on package.

4. Get your glasses and beverages in place, and put your flatware, napkins, salt, pepper, and butter out on the table.

5. Everything should be ready by now. Take the baguette out now. Give it a few minutes before you slice. Hold baguette with a dish towel when you slice so as not to burn your hands. Place baguette pieces into a bread basket lined with a pretty cloth napkin or dishcloth, and cover the bread with the cloth. Either place the vegetables onto plates or have everyone serve themselves. Do the same with the rice and parsley. Enjoy your meal, have everyone help clean up, and then enjoy your choice of ice cream bars with very little additional clean up. You have an easy, simple, and delicious home cooked meal. Now you can move on to something more detailed. This is a great first meal for your kiddos to learn to prepare, and it is one of my "go-tos" for a busy day.

Beef Stew in the Slow Cooker

Beef Stew in the slow cooker to come home to at the end of a hectic day. Here, served on Wedgewood China with pretty table linens, can elevate an ordinary weeknight dinner into something special.

6 SERVINGS

There is nothing like coming home to a home cooked meal that is already prepared. Using a slow cooker is a nice way to have a meal ready when you arrive home. This recipe just has you adding some corn starch and parsley near the end so that's really the only thing you need to do. Set the table, get your drinks and glasses out, and have a meal ready shortly after your ETA. Sometimes, I substitute sweet potatoes for the white potatoes. It adds a slightly different taste, but I like it. Sweet potatoes are so good for you, being high in potassium and vitamin A. Another variation is to skip the potatoes all together and serve over store-bought mashed potatoes, like Bob Evans. Prepare packaged mashed potatoes as directed on the package, spoon into bowls, and ladle beef stew over the mashed potatoes. This is a really nice hearty and healthy meal.

2 pounds of stew meat trimmed and cut into 1-inch cubes

2 ½ cups white potatoes peeled and cubed (If substituting sweet potatoes, use 1 cup, as sweet potatoes add more flavor.)

2 cups carrots cut into 1-½ inch pieces

1 ¼ cups chopped white onions

2 cups of canned tomato sauce

1 ½ cups of beef broth

3 cloves of garlic, finely chopped

1 tablespoon Dijon mustard

1 ¼ dried thyme or 1 tablespoon of fresh thyme

1 teaspoon sugar

½ teaspoon sea salt

½ teaspoon freshly ground black pepper

1 tablespoon cornstarch or flour

½ cup fresh parsley chopped

1. Combine all ingredients except for the corn starch/flour and parsley in a slow cooker, at least 3 quarts in size.

2. Cover and simmer on your low setting for about 9 hours. Stir occasionally.

3. Combine corn starch/flour with 1 tablespoon of water and stir with a fork or mini-whisk until free of lumps. Add this to stew and cook for an additional 45 minutes to an hour.

4. Add in and stir parsley, just before serving. Enjoy!

Bolognese Sauce and Pasta

Bolognese with Pasta served with fruit, vegetables in season and a frozen baguette from the grocery store, heated as you put finishing touches on the table, fresh flowers, water in old colored wine bottles and "Riuniti on ice...tastes so nice!"

5-6 SERVINGS

Everyone needs a good tomato-based pasta sauce. Once you start making your own, you can suit it to your needs and those gathering around your table, adding or omitting the vegetables you don't have on hand or don't prefer. I use spaghetti and linguini pasta less than I used to. I like shell or orecchiette because they are thicker and soak up more of the sauce, but use your favorite.

Olive oil to coat your pan

¼ cup chopped onion

1 pound ground beef (I like sirloin.)

3 cloves finely chopped garlic

½ cup chopped celery

½ cup chopped carrot

1 teaspoon fresh oregano

⅛ teaspoon crushed red pepper flakes

1 cup dry red wine

1-28 ounce can crushed tomatoes

3 tablespoons tomato paste

1 teaspoon sea salt

½ teaspoon freshly ground black pepper

1-12 ounce package Orecchiette (Orecchiette means shaped like little ears.)

¼ cup fresh basil leaves chopped

¼ cup freshly chopped parsley

1/3 cup freshly grated Parmesan cheese

1. Heat your olive oil in a large saute' pan, or I like using a LeCreuset Dutch oven because the sauce doesn't make as much of a mess on the stove. Add the chopped onion. When onion is translucent, add the ground beef, stirring with a wooden spoon.

2. When ground beef is no longer pink, add the celery and carrots. When they are soft, add the garlic, red pepper flakes, and oregano.

3. Pour the wine in and stir, scraping the bottom. Now add the crushed tomatoes, tomato paste, salt, and pepper. Stir until combined. Bring to a boil, turn heat down, and simmer for about 8 minutes.

4. Cook pasta as directed, drain and set aside.

5. Add the basil and parsley to the sauce while the pasta is cooking, and then stir in the Parmesan cheese. Add the drained pasta, and toss together.

6. Serve into a bowl or plate, and top with additional grated Parmesan cheese if desired.

Chicken McMama

Chicken McMama here alongside acorn squash baked with maple syrup and a little unsalted butter, with steamed broccoli, Michigan toast, dry red wine, candles and a fire. A lovely cold weather meal.

6 SERVINGS

When my kids were at home, this was one of their favorites and mine for a few reasons. Made with thin chicken breast meat or tenders, it is a very easy dinner or lunch. It can be packed up in a lunch for the next day. In my home economics class I teach for children, this would be one of the favorite dinners/lunches we cook. Have some honey or BBQ sauce for dipping, and you won't miss the fast-food version.

1 package of thin chicken breast meat (usually 4 count) or tenders

Milk to soak the chicken

½ cup bread crumbs *

⅓ cup grated fresh Parmesan cheese

1 teaspoon finely chopped fresh parsley

¼ teaspoon freshly ground black pepper

1. Place the chicken in a bowl or glass dish. (I use a glass bread pan.) Pour enough milk to cover the chicken and let sit for at least 30 minutes in the refrigerator. Preheat your oven to 375 degrees.

2. In a pie plate, mix the bread crumbs, Parmesan cheese, parsley, and pepper with a fork. Line a cookie sheet/baking pan with parchment paper.

3. Dip the chicken pieces in the breading mixture, coating each piece quite well on all sides. Place chicken on a parchment-lined baking sheet pan.

4. Bake the chicken about 15-20 minutes depending on your oven. Serve with a good side dish mentioned in Chapter 5 or a steamed vegetable.

*Bread crumbs

I make my own with bread from the day before. I toast it, let it cool. Then place it in the blender or food processor to turn to crumbs. Make sure the toast is cool so that the steam from the warmed toast doesn't create moisture that would make a mess. Store leftover bread crumbs in the freezer in freezer bags.

Grilled Lamb Chops

Grilled Lamb Chops, acorn squash again, Quinoa Salad (chapter 5) and Michigan Toast, served on the round drop leaf re-sale shop table in the sunroom.

2 CHOPS PER PERSON

Lamb Chops are fairly easy to find in the grocery store, and I prepare them for dinner frequently. With a good side dish, like one of those in chapter 4, your own, or a steamed vegetable with some mint jelly on the side, you have a very delicious dinner in not a lot of time.

Lamb chops

Mint jelly if desired

1. Preheat your grill.

2. Dry lamb chops. I like to brush the grill grates with olive oil so the lamb chops don't stick.

3. When grill is hot, cook each side for 2-3 minutes or until desired doneness. Lamb chops are usually served medium rare, but that is just a suggestion.

4. Plate with a vegetable or side dish and mint jelly on the side.

Michigan Toast

Michigan Toast. A nice accompaniment to any meal when one does not have freshly baked bread on hand.

1-2 SLICES PER PERSON

I started making Michigan Toast for dinner when the kids were little. We would go out for dinner, and many restaurants offered a "Texas Toast," as a bread option. I thought to myself, why can't I make our own version and call it "Michigan Toast"? And here it is. I usually make it with bread that is a day or two older than freshly baked. It's almost as good as fresh bread ... almost.

White bread or Brioche, sliced about 3/4 inch thick

Unsalted butter, softened to room temperature

Garlic salt

Ground Cayenne red pepper or paprika

1. Preheat oven to 375 degrees.

2. While oven heats, spread unsalted butter onto slices of bread. Place on a cookie sheet or baking pan.

3. Sprinkle garlic salt on the buttered slices. Lightly dust paprika, or for a little heat use ground Cayenne red pepper.

4. Toast in the oven for about 5 minutes, depending on your oven.

5. Take out of oven and place in a bread basket lined with a pretty napkin.

Chapter 3
It's a Great Day To...
Happy Hour? Why Not?

Some nights, a sit-down dinner is just not going to work. Everyone is going in different directions or your time together only overlaps for a short period. Likewise, coordinating a dinner with Friends or neighbors is hard to make happen. This is when I like to call for a HAPPY HOUR. It need not be alcoholic, although it can be. Sometimes, it's easier to gather people for a short period of time.

Some neighbors and I get together like this. If we haven't seen one another for a while, one of us will text and say something like *"Haven't seen you all in a while. How about HAPPY HOUR tomorrow at 4:30ish?"* What this involves is stopping by the hostess's house for a 4:30-6:00ish get-together of whatever snacks the hostess has on hand. No one brings anything. We just get together, catch up, and go home. That's it! We just like to check in with one another to see what we all have been up to. We have also done this with a group before going out to dinner to a favorite restaurant. Everyone comes over an hour or so before we need to leave for a dinner reservation. Sometimes when sitting around a table in a restaurant, you don't get to catch up with someone at the other end of a table, or you can't hear adequately because of the background noise. So during a HAPPY HOUR, you can walk around and talk to everyone. There is not a big time commitment in preparation. You keep it simple because you'll be having dinner. It's just an opportunity to get the evening started and see good Friends or Family to re-connect. LOVE THAT!

This concept can work for a simple dinner too. Think about an easily prepared meal, like a make-your-own-sandwich bar with what is on hand from the fridge/pantry; or a Chicken Noodle Soup made with a rotisserie chicken from the grocery store, chicken stock, noodles, and veggies on hand; fresh fruit or a salad; and an unbaked baguette from the grocery as well, baked for 10-12 minutes at home while everything is being prepared. This easy dinner can be enjoyed around an island or counter in the kitchen. Everyone stands around or sits at counter stools. It's easy to prepare, easy to enjoy, everyone cleans up, and then goes their separate ways on a busy night. It's not that hard and is great way to connect. It gets you to "Gather Around a Table (Counter or Island)."

Mary Yana's Happy Hour Recipe

White platter, your favorite platter, large or small, create your own style of an impromptu Happy Hour, based on what you like and what you have on hand. Make it simple and easy so YOU are happy. Isn't that the whole point?

8-10 SERVINGS (OR MANY MORE)

1. A HOME that is set up "Company Ready"
   Guest bath/powder room always clean and tidy
   Front porch looking spiffy

2. Your favorite candles on hand
   Target Magnolia Home - Fig, Poppy
   Williams Sonoma - Lavender, Grapefruit Lemon
   Bath and Body Works - Midnight Blue Citrus
   Anthropologie - Capri Blue Volcano Candle

3. Foods to have on hand
   Cream Cheese/Red Pepper Jelly or Onion Jelly
   Your Favorite Crackers- (I like Triscuits), Corn Chips (I like blue, but your Favorite are the best)
   Fruit (I like berries because they are easy to eat)
   Nuts (cashews, honey roasted peanuts or raw)
   Veggies (carrot and celery sticks - soak in water to store, mini tomatoes)
   Cheese (cut into little chunks) your Favorites

4. Drinks (Remember who your guests are, kids/adults/both)
   Club soda or flavored non-alcoholic sparkling water
   Sweet Tea/Lemonade with Agave
   Your Favorite beer
   Favorite wines (a white and red)

An Easy Summer Drink
(For me, Sangria or Lambrusco served with lots of ice)

5. Garnishes for drinks
   Lemons, limes, and oranges

6. Serving items
   Paper or cloth napkins
   Paper plates or your everyday dishes (little plates)
   Plastic or glass cups
   Your Favorite serving platters
   (I like white because the food stands out. I also use colorful ones.)

7. Look Your Best! (Get yourself ready first.)
   Know what your Favorites are (dress, jeans, t-shirt, top, earrings)
   Comfy shoes or flip flops
   Your fragrance
   Easy make-up

8. Music
   Have a soundtrack of music that makes you feel FABULOUS!
   Play this music while you are getting yourself ready for your gathering, in the car, and on a bad day.
   This is not hard, but it takes a little work and some practice. You will become more comfortable each time you do it. Entertaining and having fun is an art.

Guacamole

Most people like guacamole. It is so easy to make. Here's an easy recipe to serve with your favorite corn chips. (I like the blue variety, but remember to have dental floss on hand for your guests.)

4-6 SERVINGS

3 ripe avocados, cut in half (Scoop out the flesh and remove the pit)

1 tablespoon fresh lime juice

4 dashes hot sauce (Tabasco or Frank's)

¼ cup finely diced purple onion

¼ teaspoon sea salt

¼ teaspoon freshly ground black pepper

⅓ cup finely diced grape or mini tomatoes

Fresh cilantro (I use about a handful of cilantro, leaves only.)

1. Gently mix the mashed avocado with the lime juice, hot sauce, sea salt, and pepper. You want this mixture to be a little lumpy, so don't over blend.

2. Now add the purple onion, tomatoes, and chopped cilantro. I like to serve immediately in a bowl next to a basket of my favorite chips. Use a few sprigs of cilantro to garnish.

Chapter 4
It's a Great Day To... Remember that
"Breakfast, the Most Important Meal of the Day?"

The phrase "Breakfast, the most important meal of the day" is up for debate, depending on which nutritionist one follows. However, most important is HOW you start your day, which is just as important as what you eat. For me, it does, in some way, begin with something to eat, so I like it to be something good that will give me energy to get me through the morning so that I can be at my best. Some form of protein: boiled eggs, cottage cheese, Greek yogurt, a slice of quiche and usually fresh fruit or a Greek yogurt smoothie with frozen berries. I usually go over my schedule for the day while I eat, make the Hubby breakfast, get myself ready, and head out myself.

A smooth morning means preparing the night before with clothes out, bag packed, etc. When the kiddos were at home, I would set the counter at night. The kids got their clothes out, all homework done and in the backpack, and backpacks by the back door and ready to go. I remember learning this skill in Brownies when I was around age 7. I wanted to do everything I could do as a parent to make sure my kids were rested, well-nourished, and ready to learn. A teacher can only do so much if home-base doesn't do its part.

When I taught school, I told my students' parents, "Send me a child that is well-rested, well-nourished, with a sense of right and wrong, and I can do wonders." I subscribed to that on the other side of the table as well. We'd have breakfast at the counter and still do. A little informal. I would usually stand on the other side getting them seconds and asking about their day ahead. Sometimes reviewing for a test or presentation, going over after school and evening plans, putting dishes in the dishwasher when finished, brushing their teeth, and then heading out the door with a kiss and a hug.

Like every other chapter and topic in this book, I am sharing my experiences and thoughts to help YOU make YOUR ROUTINE YOURS. There is no right or wrong here. Sometimes situations fit into a routine organically. Maybe it's because your parents did or didn't do something that you do things the way you do. We are creatures of habit, and once you decide on your routine, it's comforting to you (and your Family) to settle into a routine and make it yours. It's in these routines, these times that we gather, either before we head out the door or when we come home, that we talk about our highs/lows, thoughts, and concerns. If it's just you at home, maybe a few times a week you meet a Friend or Friends. Once in a while, I meet a Friend at a local coffee/bagel shop. The place is always busy. I see the same groups of people meeting. They all look happy, and they sit for quite a while. That is their routine. Think about your routine, and if you are not happy with it, change it. Ask yourself, "What WOULD help me get my day off to a good start?" Then make it happen. Just a few thoughts and here are a few of my favorite things for breakfast to help make it a Great Day.

Blueberry Yogurt Smoothie

Everything you need for a delicious breakfast-on-the-go or pick-me-up snack.

1 SERVING

If you are on the go, a smoothie is a good choice. Just make sure if you are on the go you have a top for your cup. The lemon juice balances with the honey and gives this a very full and substantial taste. Yum!

½ cup of frozen blueberries

1 tablespoon freshly squeezed lemon juice

1 tablespoon honey

½ cup skim milk

½ cup plain Greek yogurt

1. Place in a blender and mix.

2. Pour into a tall glass.

Eggs to Order

Eggs to order. A great way to start or end the day. To shake things up every once in a while, consider "breakfast for dinner."

SERVINGS: 2 EGGS PER PERSON

t's good to know how to prepare eggs in a variety of ways. Serve your eggs with your favorite toast/ English muffins and fruit to get your day (or someone you love) off to a great start.

1. Boiled Eggs - Place your eggs in a saucepan. Fill pan with water (about an inch of water above the eggs) and bring water to a rapid boil over high heat. Turn the heat off once the water reaches boiling. Now cover the saucepan with the lid. Remove from the heat and let sit for 10-12 minutes for hard-boiled. After that time, pour the water out of the pan and fill with cold water. Serve or place in the refrigerator to be enjoyed later.

2. Scrambled Eggs - Heat a frying pan and melt unsalted butter. Crack eggs separately in small bowl, then pour into a larger bowl as not to get shells in the mix. Add about a ½ tablespoon of milk per egg. Beat with a fork or whisk. When pan is hot, pour egg mixture in. Scramble as they cook to desired doneness and serve immediately. An egg or egg white substitute can also be used.

3. Fried/Over Easy Eggs - Heat frying pan and melt unsalted butter. Crack each egg individually into the pan. Let egg yolk set, and flip. Cook until desired doneness.

Let's Have a Party Quiche

Party Quiche smells glorious in the oven while it bakes. I love a piece of Party Quiche reheated in the oven-rather than the microwave-for breakfast.

8 SERVINGS

When I was in high school, I worked at the local library a few days after school and on Saturdays. One of the librarians had us over in December for a very lovely Christmas Party that she spent weeks preparing for. My recipe is a variation of the delicious quiche that was served at that party. I have not tasted a quiche since then that has this blend of flavors.

2 eggs beaten

1 cup Hellmann's Mayonnaise

2 tablespoons unbleached flour

½ cup skim milk

4 ounces shredded cheddar cheese

4 ounces shredded Swiss or Gruyere

1 ¼ cup of washed and sliced mushrooms of your choice

½ pkg. (envelope) Lipton's Onion Soup Mix

1 small (10-ounce package) frozen spinach, thawed and drained

1. Mix beaten eggs, mayonnaise, flour, and milk.

2. Add the powdered Lipton Onion Soup Mix, cheeses, mushrooms, and thawed spinach.

3. Pour into a prepared store-bought or homemade crust (see below). I like a 12-inch quiche dish.

4. Bake for 40-50 minutes, checking doneness after 40 minutes. Reset timer if placing quiche back into oven for additional baking time. Let cool before slicing. I like to place leftover small slices into doubled freezer bags. Best if warmed in a 375-degree oven, check after 5 minutes.

Quiche Crust

1 ¼ cup unbleached flour

½ teaspoon Kosher salt

½ teaspoon white granular sugar

1 stick (8 tablespoons) unsalted butter, cut up into small pieces

1-2 tablespoons cold water

1. Place dry ingredients into the bowl of a stand mixer and blend.

2. When well blended, add small pieces of butter, a few pieces at a time. When crumbly, add water, a small amount at a time until dough looks to be a consistency that will roll well.

3. Roll onto a floured pastry cloth and place into a 12-inch quiche dish. Fill with quiche mixture.

Chapter 5
It's a Great Day To... Have
Lunch on the Go... or at Home

It's fun to meet Friends out for lunch to catch up, but most of the time, I have lunch at home. If I have a busy day out, I often pack my lunch in a little cooler to eat at a park, in the car, or wherever I can find a nice spot. Keeping good food on hand and having a soup or salad in the fridge makes this easy. I usually have some type of salad and/or a soup on hand (soup almost always in the fall/winter/early spring). Another benefit is it makes it easy to have a Friend over at the last minute. Many positives of this, but most importantly, you know what you are eating. You can season it the way you want, and with a little preparation, you have several good lunches, afternoon pick-me-ups or an easy dinner side dish to serve alongside a piece of salmon, grilled chicken, or steak on the grill. Here are a few of my Favorite easy lunches with many possibilities to eat solo or to find someone to ... "Gather Around a Table" with.

Grilled Cheese Sandwiches

Who doesn't love a simple and delicious grilled cheese sandwich? Serve alone or here pictured with my favorite soup, M.Y. Healthy Cream of Butternut Squash Soup and a Strong Bow, my favorite British Cider.

1 SERVING

When I lived at Martha Cook, the all-girls dorm at the University of Michigan, one of my four very close Friends' favorite lunches was grilled cheese and tomato soup. She loved that lunch and enjoyed it every time it was on the menu. When our kids were old enough to eat grilled cheese sandwiches, I introduced them to not only grilled cheese, but to other varieties of grilled sandwiches ... ham and cheese, peanut butter, white cheddar with onion jam, and mozzarella/tomato/basil. One can become so creative with grilled sandwiches, switching up the bread, the cheese, and the other fixings. Here are the basics, and you can take off from here. The sky's the limit with this old standby. Enjoy!

Unsalted butter at room temperature
Good quality bread like Brioche, white, sour-dough or your favorite

Basic (Cheddar cheese) 2-3 slices.

Grilled Ham and Cheese (sliced ham and Cheddar or Swiss cheese). I like two slices of cheese with 1-2 slices of ham in between.

Grilled Cheddar with Onion Jam (white Cheddar and Onion jam). 1-2 slices of white cheddar with a light layer of Onion jam. Too much will make the sandwich messy. American Spoon makes a good one and Brasswell's makes a good one, too, usually found in the grocery store.

Grilled Italian Sandwich (Sliced Mozzarella cheese - fresh basil leaves, sliced tomatoes). 2 slices of Mozzarella, with a slice of a ripe tomato and 3 basil leaves in between the cheese.

Grilled Peanut Butter Sandwich. Spread a light to medium layer of a smooth peanut butter between the two slices of bread.

1. Place grill pan on stove and turn to medium heat.

2. Place sandwich, buttered side down, in the grill pan. Lower heat just a little, and place lid on top to allow the cheese on the sandwiches to get soft.

3. In about 3-5 minutes, take cover off, spread butter likewise on the other side of the sandwich and flip the sandwich over. Place the lid on once again for another 3-5 minutes. A grilled sandwich is nicely paired with my Healthy Cream of Squash Soup.

Tuna Salad Sandwiches

A Tuna Salad ready to take in to the Hubby working from home, like so many of the pandemic days.

4 SERVINGS

My husband and I were married almost 30 years before I discovered he liked tuna fish sandwiches. Like the previous Grilled Cheese Sandwiches, there is some variety when one opens a can of tuna fish. I like the Albacore variety, and of the Albacore, I like the wild-caught, and of the wild-caught, I prefer canned in water. Got all that? I make the salad, place it between two slices of my favorite bread (which usually is Brioche) for a sandwich for the Hubby, and for a salad, I scoop the tuna mixture on a bed of lettuce or spinach for me. Sometimes I want the basic tuna salad, made with mayonnaise, and to switch it up, I'll make a white bean version with a vinaigrette. Totally different but equally satisfying. Perfect for lunch at home or on the go. Just remember, if taking the mayonnaise version, you want to store it in a cooler lunch box with a chilling ice pack from the freezer. Although you could serve the white bean version on bread, it might be filling. This one is best served on a plate rather than in a sandwich.

Basic Tuna Salad

1 large can wild-caught Albacore tuna packed in water and drained

2 stalks of celery, trimmed and chopped finely

¼ cup chopped white onion

2 to 2 ½ tablespoons Hellman's Mayonnaise

Optional: chopped fresh curly parsley

Sea salt and freshly ground black pepper to taste

1. Mix all together.

2. Serve either on bread for a sandwich or alone over a bed of lettuce.

3. Makes enough for two, and then have some on hand, stored in an airtight container in the refrigerator for a couple days.

Italian White Bean Tuna Salad

1-12 ounce can wild caught Albacore tuna packed in water and drained

1 can white cannellini beans drained and rinsed

¼ cup thinly sliced purple onions

¼ cup multi-colored mini-tomatoes, whole

1 bunch flat leaf, Italian parsley, leaves only (Cut stems off and chop.)

1 tablespoon red wine vinegar

Sea salt and freshly ground black pepper

Mix together and serve. Store leftovers in an airtight container for a couple of days in the refrigerator.

Quinoa and Fresh Vegetables

Quinoa and Fresh Vegetable Salad. It is nice to have in the fridge for lunch, a snack, side dish at dinner or in a container for lunch on the go. Don't forget the dental floss.

6-8 SERVINGS

Quinoa has become very popular over the past few years. I prefer the red quinoa simply because I like the contrast in color with the color of the fresh vegetables. Although I frequently use quinoa for this salad, it is equally good with the ancient grain, Farro, a larger and chewier grain. The dressing has a nice tangy taste. This dish can be served as a salad alone for a lunch or as a side dish for dinner.

2 cups cooked, drained, and cooled quinoa (or Farro)

¼ cup carrots diced

¼ cup green pepper diced

¼ cup diced red pepper

½ cup chopped parsley

¼ cup scallions diced

¼ cup mini tomatoes diced

Dressing

½ cup canola oil

½ cup low sodium soy sauce

3 tablespoons red wine vinegar

2 teaspoons Dijon mustard

1. Mix together, gently stirring grain and vegetables. Set aside.

2. Whisk all of the dressing ingredients with a fork or mini whisk.

3. Pour slowly over grain and vegetable mixture, occasionally stopping to incorporate the dressing into the salad. If using the quinoa, it will take less dressing because the grain is less dense. The Farro will need more of the mixed dressing. Go very lightly on the dressing, as you can add more.

4. Store leftovers in the fridge and enjoy for a few days.

Tabbouli

I like to take Tabbouli when asked to bring a salad to a gathering. Here I am ready to go, along with my Homemade Basic White Bread (chapter 6).

6-8 SERVINGS

Tabbouli is a Middle-Eastern salad, originating in Lebanon and Syria. Some recipes are heavier on the parsley, and some are heavier on the bulgur wheat. Here is a basic recipe. Depending on your preferences, you may want to make it heavier in one or the other. However you make it, just be sure to have dental floss on hand to get the parsley out from between your teeth or those of your guests.

1 cup bulgur wheat (dry)

2 cups boiling water

1 cup finely chopped grape tomatoes (I like the colorful variety, but any will do.)

1 bunch of scallions, with tops finely chopped after trimming off dry ends

2 bunches curly parsley, finely chopped (Use the flowery part, not much of the stalks/stems.)

Optional: 3 tablespoons mint leaves, chopped

Dressing

½ cup lemon juice preferable fresh squeezed

4 tablespoons olive oil

½ teaspoon sea salt

¼ teaspoon freshly ground black pepper

1. In a medium bowl, soak the dry bulgur wheat in the boiling water for about 1 hour. Drain well, pressing out the water through a strainer or cloth. In a larger bowl, add all of the other vegetables and stir to mix. Mix up the dressing in a bowl with a small whisk or fork. Blend the vegetables and the drained bulgur wheat.

2. No more than one hour prior to serving, add the dressing gradually. You do not want to make it too soggy, and you may not use all of the dressing, depending on how "dressed" you prefer your Tabbouli to be.

3. Fluff/stir again before serving. If there is any left after serving, store for a day or two in the fridge, tightly covered.

Cream of Butternut Squash Soup

Healthy Cream of Butternut Squash Soup, served alongside a grilled sandwich, here in a jam jar with fresh ground black pepper.

6-8 SERVINGS

This soup has a rich, creamy taste; however, the fullness of this soup gets its flavor from lots of puréed squash and skim milk, rather than heavy cream. There is a healthy food chain that carries a Butternut Squash that is overly sweet. This one is not. I have substituted cauliflower for the Butternut Squash. It is a nice soup to accompany a sandwich or a salad like, Tabbouli or MY Farro Salad. This soup freezes quite well, so if you have leftover soup after your lunch, freeze it in freezer bags or freezer containers in individual servings so you can enjoy it at a later time.

1 tablespoon unsalted butter

½ cup chopped white onion

3 cloves minced garlic

¼ teaspoon freshly ground pepper (I like a little extra for a peppery taste.)

2 ½ cups chicken stock (I use chicken the product, "Better than Bouillon," found in the soup aisle in the grocery store near the boxed stocks and broths.)

3 pounds Butternut squash, peeled, seeded, peeled and chopped into small cubes

1 ½-2 cups skim milk

1. In a stockpot, melt the unsalted butter and sauté the onions until translucent. Add the garlic and cook an additional minute.

2. Add the salt, pepper, broth, and squash. Bring the liquid to a boil. Turn heat down and simmer for 8 minutes or until soft.

3. Turn the heat off, remove pot from the burner and stir in the skim milk.

4. Purée the soup with an immersion hand blender or carefully pour the soup into a blender. Return soup to the pot and heat before serving. Do not boil.

Chapter 6
It's a Great Day To...
"Let Them Eat Cake"...
(or any dessert)

When Marie Antoinette made this clueless comment, she had no regard for the common people of France who were starving. The word she used was actually "Brioche." In my context, I am referring to the ideas of "Why not eat dessert?" Now, not a whole plate of cookies or half a pie, but a little dessert in moderation is a good thing, I think. If you are going to enjoy a treat, eat something good and have something delicious to enjoy on hand. Again, if you make it yourself, you know what is in it, and you have more control of what you are eating. I like to have some homemade cookies (or good store-bought ones) in a cake dome/plate on the counter. I think everyone needs a good cookie recipe in their repertoire if you don't already have one.

When I was growing up, everyone loved their mom's version of chocolate chip cookies. A Friend of mine is known for her Scotcheroos, and she often brings them to a gathering when asked to bring a dish. THEY ARE THE BEST. She didn't create the recipe, but we all associate her with them. So what's your dish/dessert? I love it when someone takes a dish and makes it their own. Think about that. I'll give you a few of my favorites, but again, in looking at my recipes, think about what yours are or how you could tinker with mine (or really any recipe) and make it yours. It is fun to know a recipe so well that it is ingrained in your mind. When you know it so well, you can edit it to make it YOURS. I often write notes in the margins of my recipes based on other recipes I have tried or had while traveling, and it's fun to see how the original has evolved. Keep track of your changes so you can duplicate it the next time you make it. More thoughts on this all later. Let's eat some cake now.

Basic White Bread and Cinnamon Bread

I have been making these two recipes for years. The white bread is my "go-to" sandwich bread and Michigan Toast bread. Usually, however not always, I make the cinnamon bread in the cooler weather. It makes a nice treat to enjoy by the fire with some hot cocoa.

12-14 SERVINGS

For the past twenty-something years, I have started yeast bread recipes with a bread machine however, I mostly use it for mixing and rising the dough because I like the look of a loaf baked in a bread pan or a round loaf, both of which are unachievable from bread baked in a bread machine. I place ingredients in the bowl of the bread machine, set it on "dough mode," take it out, when done, knead or roll into a rectangle, place into a buttered loaf pan, let it rise, bake it and enjoy!

For Basic White Bread

2 ¼ teaspoons of yeast

3 cups of unbleached flour

1 ½ tablespoons sugar

1 teaspoon kosher salt

1 cup plus 2 tablespoons water, warmed in the microwave for 50 seconds (warm but not too hot is what you want)

2 tablespoons unsalted butter (warmed in the microwave for 30 seconds)

1. Place all ingredients in the bowl of the bread machine in this order and turn on. Mine usually takes 2 hours 35 minutes.

2. Preheat oven to 350 degrees.

3. Divide dough into 2 and shape into 2 loaves and placing into buttered loaf pans.

4. Cover bread pans with plastic wrap and place in a warm area to rise until doubled in bulk (about 30-40 minutes, depending on your yeast, room temperature and kitchen conditions.) I like to place the bread under the hood lights and place on top of the stove, making sure no burner are on.

5. Remove plastic and bake for 30-35 minutes.

6. Cool for about 5 minutes in pans on a wire rack and then remove from pans.

For Cinnamon Bread

¼ cup granulated sugar

1 ¼ teaspoons cinnamon

2 tablespoons unsalted butter

1. Combine the granulated sugar and cinnamon in a bowl and set aside.

2. Melt the unsalted butter in the microwave for about 25 seconds.

3. Roll each half of the dough, into a rectangle on a floured surface. I like to use a pastry cloth.

4. Brush rectangle with melted butter.

5. Sprinkle half of the cinnamon sugar mixture onto each buttered rectangular piece of dough.

6. Roll the dough and place seam onto bottom of the bread pan.

7. Repeat process with second ball of dough.

8. Place plastic wrap over each bread pan and place in a warm place to rise. I like to turn hood lights on and place on top of stove, making sure no burners are on.

9. Preheat oven to 350 degrees.

10. When dough is approximately doubled in bulk (about 30-40 minutes rise time, depending on your yeast, room temperature, and kitchen conditions),

11. Remove plastic wrap and place both bread pans into preheated oven with space between each pan.

12. Bake for 30-35 minutes until crust is browned. Remove from oven, place on wire rack for 5 minutes, and then remove bread from pan to cool on rack, if you can wait.

Mary Yana's French Brioche

I have tried several Brioche recipes and developed my own, mixing and letting the dough rise in the bread machine. This is my SPECIAL BREAD that I take to my SPECIAL PEOPLE.

APPROXIMATELY 20 SERVINGS

I have been baking Brioche for about 14 years. When Melanie, our foreign exchange student from Perpignan in the southeast of France, came to stay with us when our kiddos were in high school, I thought I should learn to make some foods from her home country. That's when my baking of Brioche began. I have used a few different recipes over the years, and here is the result of all I have learned.

When my bread machine broke, I decided not to replace it and just use it for mixing the dough and the first rising of bread. I like the look of bread baked in an "official" bread pan rather than the usual bread machine pan. Don't forget the egg wash at the end. I have done that more than once, and although it is not absolutely necessary, it does result in a pretty shiny crust which Brioche is known for. Enjoy!

2 ½ teaspoons of yeast in a jar (or 1 pkg, which is a little less than that, but will do)

4 ¼ cups of unbleached flour

½ cup of water warmed in the microwave for about 30 seconds

3 tablespoons granulated sugar

6 extra-large eggs at room temperature (place in warm water in a bowl to speed up the process)

2 teaspoons kosher salt

2 sticks (½ pound) of unsalted butter warmed in a bowl in the microwave for about 10 seconds

1 additional egg whisked with 1 tablespoon milk for the egg wash

1. Place all ingredients in the bowl of a bread machine, placing the yeast in first, followed by the unbleached flour. The rest of the ingredients can be placed in any order after these two.

2. Hold off on mixing up the egg wash until ready to bake later.

3. Turn bread machine on dough mode, which is usually around 2 hours 35 minutes. Near the end of that time, prepare your pans and area to shape the dough.

4. Butter your bread pans with additional butter. Spread butter up high on the pan because the egg wash can make your dough stick to your pan, making it harder to get your loaf out of the pan. I like to use a little baggie to spread the butter.

5. Remove dough when cycle is completed. Turn dough onto a floured surface. Lightly knead and shape into a long loaf. Now, cut dough into two or three loaves. I place clear plastic wrap on the loaf pans and let them rise in a warm place. I like to turn on the hood light(s) and let it rise on an unused stove with no burners on. At this time, adjust your racks if necessary while oven is cool. Then preheat the oven to 375 degrees.

6. Let your dough rise until approximately doubled in bulk. Just before that point, mix your egg with 1 tablespoon of water. Remove the clear plastic wrap, brush the top of each loaf with the egg wash, and place in the oven, leaving space in the oven between the loaf pans. If baking three loaves, start checking your bread through the oven window at about 32 minutes, looking for a browned crust. For two slightly larger loaves, check them at about 36 minutes. Ovens can vary in temperature slightly, so the first time you make the Brioche, take note and refer back for the next time. Remember to reset your timers so your bread does not burn. Bread is done when tapped and sounds a bit hollow. Have a wire rack handy to turn loves out onto to cool. If there is any left over, I like to slice it before placing it in a freezer bag so I can get a single slice out to toast, when necessary. Remember, if toasting Brioche, it browns quicker than regular bread because of the high butter content, so set your toaster accordingly.

Berry Cobbler

Berry Cobbler...Delicious!

6 SERVINGS

I f I am entertaining or asked to bring a dessert to a gathering in the late spring or summer months, this is usually my first choice. I like a fruit cobbler (blueberry or raspberry) because it involves a top crust only, which means less time and fewer calories. Frozen raspberries can be substituted as well. Also, when one goes to the effort to make a delicious dessert like this, one MUST serve a dollop of fresh whipped cream on top. Just delicious!

Crust

1 cup unbleached flour

1 ½ teaspoons granulated sugar

⅛ teaspoon sea salt

1 stick unsalted butter, cold and cut into small cubes

Fruit Filling

20 ounces frozen raspberries or blueberries

⅓ cup sugar plus some to sprinkle on top of crust

Whipping Cream

½ pint whipping cream

2 teaspoons granulated sugar

1. Preheat oven to 425 degrees.

2. Place the flour, sugar, and salt in either the bowl of a stand mixer or a food processor and blend.

3. Add the butter cut into small pieces and blend until the mixture resembles a course meal. Add enough ice water, only a few drops at a time, to hold the dough together. Remove the dough from the mixer and shape into a thick disk. Wrap in plastic wrap and refrigerate for about 10 minutes.

4. Place the frozen berries into a baking dish measuring about 5 x 10 inches. Sprinkle with the 3 tablespoons of sugar evenly.

5. Place the uncovered disk of dough onto a floured surface. (I like to use a pastry cloth.) Sprinkle with flour and roll out to a shape a little larger than your baking dish. Place the rolled dough onto the top of the berries topped with sugar. Shape/crimp the edges and cut a decorative pattern in the crust. Brush crust with ½ tablespoon whipping cream and sprinkle with granulated sugar. Prick crust with a fork a few times for air to release while baking. Bake until the crust is a golden-brown color and juices are bubbling, which will be about 25 minutes.

6. Whip cream with a mixer starting slowly and speeding up as the cream gets thicker. Add the 2 teaspoons of granulated sugar and mix until cream is fluffy and smooth.

7. Serve cobbler with a dollop or two of whipped cream.

Cutout Cookies

When I help out in classrooms a recipe of these cookies almost always comes along with me, in shapes pertaining to the lesson. The kids love these. Wouldn't they make you smile?

3 DOZEN SERVINGS

Of all the cookie recipes I have made during my married life, this would be the recipe I have made the most. The recipe is from my husband's mother, who in turn got the recipe from her Friend who received the recipe during her education as a home economics teacher at Michigan State University during the late 1950s. There are three reasons why this is a favorite of mine. One, unlike many other cutout cookie recipes, it does not need to be refrigerated before rolling. Two, it contains no eggs, so if a little person decides to sneak some while you are not looking, there is not the concern of ingesting raw eggs. Thirdly, they are so delicious. I like to roll them thin (so you can enjoy a couple extra) and sprinkle with pretty colored sugars, depending on the season. You may find that once you get into the habit of making these during the holidays and special occasions, you may find yourself frequently on the lookout for unique cookie cutters that have significance in the lives of you and the people with whom you gather around a table.

2 sticks unsalted butter at room temperature

1 cup powdered sugar

1 teaspoon vanilla

2 ½ cups unbleached flour

2 tablespoons milk

1. Preheat oven to 325 degrees.

2. Cream unsalted butter and powdered sugar in the bowl of a mixer.

3. Add vanilla.

4. When all is well blended, add flour a little at a time until all is added.

5. Add the 2 tablespoons of milk as you add the flour to make the mixture moist and not too dry.

6. Divide into two balls of dough. Roll one ball at a time. Roll dough thin.

7. Cut with cutters and place onto a parchment-lined pan.

8. Sprinkle with colored sugar if desired. Bake for 8-10 minutes if dough is rolled thin, 10-12 minutes is rolled a bit thicker.

9. Let cool on a wire rack. Enjoy!

Baked Custard

When someone is feeling a little under the weather in our Family, they usually request a recipe of Custard.

6 SERVINGS

This is a comfort food dessert. If someone is sick at our house or a Friend or extended Family member is under the weather, Baked Custard is a good choice to offer. When one of the kids would come home for a break during their college years, Baked Custard was usually sitting on a baking rack, cooling when they walked in the door. Although I use 2% milk, skim or whole can be used as well.

2 ½ cups 2% milk

3 eggs

⅓ cup granulated sugar

1 teaspoon vanilla

Dash of salt

1. Preheat oven to 350 degrees.

2. Scald milk in the microwave, in a large Pyrex measuring cup. Warm for about 2 minutes 40 seconds.

3. While it is scalding, get 6 custard dishes ready and place custard dishes in a 9 x 13 Pyrex glass dish.

4. Measure out sugar and salt. Crack eggs and place in a custard dish.

5. When milk is scalded in microwave, remove, add granulated sugar while milk is hot and beat with a fork or whisk until sugar is dissolved.

6. Add the eggs, salt, and vanilla, and continue to beat until mixed well.

7. Pour mixture into six custard dishes and prepare hot water for the hot water bath in the Pyrex 9 x 13 baking dish. Pour the hot water into the Pyrex baking dish with all of the full custard dishes.

8. If desired, sprinkle a small amount of nutmeg on top of each filled custard dish before baking.

9. Bake for 35-40 minutes. Take out when custard is firm, and let cool before removing from hot water bath. Be careful as the hot water bath is HOT. Enjoy!

Applesauce

Homemade Applesauce does not last long at our house.

10-12 SERVINGS

Once the weather starts getting cooler and the local apples start harvesting, I get in the mood to make applesauce. Once you make it and appreciate the taste of homemade applesauce, it may just become part of your fall routine. Applesauce is on my Thanksgiving menu. I think you will like it and feel it is worth the effort. I like using different varieties of apples to vary the flavor, depending on what is available.

4 tablespoons unsalted butter cut into pieces

6 pounds of a variety of apples (approximately 16 apples)

¼ cup brown sugar

Juice and zest of 1 orange

1 ½ teaspoons cinnamon

¼ teaspoon allspice

1. Preheat oven to 350 degrees.

2. Wash, dry, peel, core, and quarter apples.

3. Place them in a large Dutch oven. Add the orange juice, zest, brown sugar, allspice, and cinnamon, and turn gently stir all ingredients.

4. Place lid on your pot and bake for about 1 ½ hours.

5. Blend with a whisk and serve warm or at room temperature.

6. Remaining applesauce should be stored in the refrigerator.

Chapter 7
It's a Great Day To...
Celebrate Holidays, Parties and Special Days

The previous chapters have mainly focused on making time to gather with ideas for our day-to-day lives. This chapter will concentrate on the "Special Days." Some of those days will be days on your calendar, days on everyone's calendar such as Easter, Passover, Christmas, Chanukah, Valentine's Day, Halloween, birthdays, graduations, and anniversaries. However, on our calendar, there have been other days to celebrate that need to be recognized. A summer party to gather with our Friends, a football party for the University of Michigan/Ohio State University Game, a Family dinner to recognize a kid getting into college, a special dinner to honor a hole in one or a tennis victory, winning a ski race, or even a special party to celebrate completing a first book, years in the making.

In seeing how we celebrate special days, my hope is that you will look at your Family's needs, traditions, and circumstances, and make your situations the best they can be. As a young wife and mother, I would sometimes see party and holiday ideas in the magazines popular at the time, and sometimes, I would feel that I didn't measure up, as if our home birthday party and traditions were not nearly as spectacular as the grand celebrations of the Hamptons, NYC, or LA, complete with petting zoos and over the top children's parties.

I could go on and on, but you get the picture. It didn't take me long to look at the big picture and see that most of the magazines are produced by people who live in big cities where life is different, not better or lesser, just different, and those people were celebrating in ways that worked for them, honoring their lives, interests, and traditions and utilizing services that were available to them. We needed to do the same. My goal is for YOU to honor those activities and fun things that YOUR PEOPLE enjoy doing in a way that works for you.

We like celebrating in our Family. I remember early on in our relationship, my husband, then my boyfriend, sent me flowers the day I got my first teaching job. He was in dental school, and we were not in the same town. On the card, he had written, "Congratulations! Let's have a special dinner to celebrate when I see you," and that was the beginning of many years of honoring "great days," and accomplishments, in addition to the holidays and days known to be celebrated.

When our first child turned one, we had a Family birthday party. When I invited my parents, my dad said, "I'll bring the hot dogs" and my mom offered to make the cake. With my dad having a Coney Island in Flint, it was very fitting for him to offer to bring the hot dogs and fixings for everyone to make their own hot dog or "Coney" as we refer to them in the Flint area. My mom offering to bring a cake was appropriate as well because she makes the best decorated cakes, and Betty Crocker Cherry Chip is our favorite flavor she makes. When I was growing up, my mom made all of our Family cakes for special occasions, and she made cakes for many of our extended Family members and neighborhood Friends.

She took a cake decorating class when I was a little girl, and she just had a talent. Every August, I would spend time pouring through her cake decorating books to get ideas for my September birthday cake. I organized the rest of the dinner. Everyone else brought their favorite dish. The party was fun. We all watched Sasha push around a little shopping cart. (Two weeks after her birthday, she walked solo.) Everyone helped clean up. It was a very nice September celebration. (She and I have birthdays one week apart.) The following year, we did the same thing, same menu, same people, every year after, even as our Family grew and the kiddos got older. Great-grandparents left us, new cousins and in-laws came into the picture, but the party menu stayed the same. We all looked forward to Sasha's September Birthday. The same idea was duplicated for Alex two years later, and then Zach six years after Alex.

We decided that we would do kid birthday parties when the kiddos turned five as well. I don't know why we decided on age five, but we just decided that was old enough. Of course, the menu was hot dogs. Grandma Diane made a cake and usually came over to help. Grandpa Jimmy brought the hot dogs, and we always had the party on a day Brad was home to run the games. He did magic tricks as well. Where did he get the idea to be home to run the party, organize games, and perform magic tricks? From his dad who did the same for his birthday parties growing up. His mom would organize his parties, and his dad was always home to help organizing the games and perform magic tricks.

The magic tricks came from something he did in the dental office to make kids at ease before they had dental work done. I remember Alex's first kid party. One of the games Brad organized was the clothespin drop into a glass milk bottle. Through the years, the games would change, but the milk bottle game stayed constant. Even as the boys became teenagers, they wanted to do it, and as we moved into a new

A cupcake made from a boxed mix, and frosting from a can, or picked up at the grocery store, a romantic December Birthday dinner, breakfast in bed, Thanksgiving Dinner with Friends and Family, Christmas Office Party at Home, Christmas morning breakfast at the kitchen counter, Christmas dinner buffet with YOUR traditional dishes.

house and they got older, they decided to do the pin drop from our second story into a slightly larger container, a pitcher. Some of the guests changed; however, one neighbor boy who came to every party every year won the pin drop every year, and every kid remembered. Those who were new each year heard about the pin drop in the weeks preceding the party, and as they all ran upstairs with excitement, they wondered if Nicholas would win again. Well, he did!

Brad recognized Nicholas's amazing hand/eye coordination early on. It is not surprising that Nicholas now has a very skilled role in the Armed Forces, where he operates detailed equipment for special services. Great memories, and it's fun to look back. You're making memories not only for your children and extended Family but for your Friends and other children, and who knows, they may be inspired to go on to make special memories for their Special People. That's pretty cool!

Holidays are fun to celebrate. However, they can be stressful and a lot of work for the person planning and executing arrangements. Holidays usually involve lots of people, lots of schedules, and lots of personalities and attitudes. I used to tell the kids that a joke is not funny unless everyone is laughing, and likewise, a party/gathering is not fun unless everyone is having fun. Some people, like me, just love it all and don't mind the work involved. I realize that I am not everyone, and everyone does not have the years of experience I have had. However, even I welcome help with clean up at times.

For a Family Holiday gathering, whether it be an official Holiday like Christmas, Chanukah, Easter, Passover, Thanksgiving, or a summer picnic holiday, most people tend to enlist help. This is nice because everyone brings a different flavor and idea, which contributes to making it easier for the host/hostess. It makes a buffet memorable and something to talk about, like a favorite aunt's ribbon Jello salad at the Fourth of July Picnic or your Mom's favorite stuffing at Thanksgiving. Everyone puts their own special touches on a dish to make it theirs.

When it comes to paper plates versus dishes, do what is best for the situation. I know a very large Family that has a very large extended Family gathering a few days before Christmas, and they do paper plates. Using paper plates allows them to have as much time visiting, catching up, and having fun with less clean up as possible. These are all very good things so that works for them. The whole point is to "Gather Around a Table," so if there is less stress to the person in charge, I am all for it.

If an event/holiday/dinner causes the person hosting to experience stress then they need some help or some short cuts. They either will not do it or will make everyone around them uncomfortable. That's so not fun. If it's your turn to host and it is not a good time for you or your Family to do so, ask for someone else to switch in the rotation. I would recommend doing this far enough in advance so as not to put another host under stress.

Carry out or catering an event if it's a large crowd for a Holiday is also an option, and one need not feel guilty or uncomfortable for utilizing that option for a special occasion or Holiday. For our son and daughter-in-law's engagement party, I hired someone to make my recipes, an idea I got from a good Friend I used to teach with. Make sure you make arrangements far enough in advance so you are able to hire someone. Call upon the services of a nice local restaurant or caterer, and they will appreciate your business. Be upfront and honest with them about the number of people you're serving and your wishes. Let them know exactly what you have in mind. There is nothing more frustrating to a business owner than a customer who does not clearly state their ideas and then the customer is disappointed because the business owner didn't read their mind. Be respectful of what is reasonable in cost and service. Most business owners aim to please, but some patrons can be unrealistic in their expectations. Treat them and everyone else with the golden rule in mind: "Treat others the way you want to be treated." That way, no one gets short-changed or taken advantage of on either end.

Remember, if you hire a caterer, you'll most likely need serving dishes, a warmer (if necessary), and serving utensils. Using your own serving dishes and utensils is a good way to put your own personal touch on a catered meal. Like in chapter one, make your table or tables look inviting with inexpensive flowers, greens from your yard, or other personal decorations. Start with the theme of the holiday or event and what you like because you'll have the flowers and decorations around the house for a while.

When getting ready for company, some people clean the house. I tend to clean or get the house cleaned AFTER the party. If you keep things tidy most of the time, all you really need to do for company is clean the bathrooms. (If you have kiddos at home, that could be their job.) Most people stay on top of the kitchen and frequently wipe down counters, faucets, and knobs. If you have kiddos at home, you can teach them to tidy bathrooms throughout the party. If we have a party, now that our kiddos are on their own, I hire teenagers to work. I give them a list of responsibilities such as cleaning the bathroom every half hour, changing towels, checking soap, wiping down everything, and emptying garbage. I have them clear plates, empty garbage, and manage coats if the celebration is during cooler months. Usually the kids wear some type of apron that I provide. I like to pay the kids in cash at the end of the evening because I want to count the money out to them so that they realize that their hard work earned them something they can hold and use how they wish. I know people like to use Venmo and other ways of payment. All are good. Just be respectful of the teenagers you employ. Like with your caterer or food provider, be clear in your expectations. I even write out a contract in advance so they know the objectives, tasks, amount they'll be paid, and time involved. That way, everyone is on the same page, and there are no surprises.

I like to respect the host's and hostess's wishes. If they ask you to bring nothing, respect that. Some hosts/hostesses have a special theme/agenda or just like doing it all because they have a vision. If you feel you'd like to do something in place of taking a dish, find out what they like or a store/coffee shop they frequent, and get them a gift card or a small gift like a dish towel, hand soap, or something homemade or from your garden like fresh herbs, vegetables, or something you have made. It doesn't have to be anything big. It could even be a nice note, phone call, or text the following day, just something to let them know you appreciate their invitation. Don't get wrapped up in the small details. Remember, people are more important than things, and do what it takes to focus on the "Gathering Around a Table" part.

In thinking about the food for your event, simple is best. If you are preparing the food, think of something that can be prepared ahead. Stews, soups, chilis, and casseroles are the easiest, I have found. Serving many items at room temperature is very popular now. I have included a few recipes for these items and a few beverages. Remember, the point is to make the Gathering and Celebration YOURS. Use these ideas if they help, but think about what YOU and YOUR Family like. What are the foods you remember having on a holiday table or picnic table? Be willing to try new traditions, but make your gathering YOURS, incorporating your Family's traditions and rituals because you are creating memories that the young people in your Family will pass on to their PEOPLE.

Turkey Chili

Turkey Chili is our unofficial college football game day at home meal, served with corn muffins or bread.

6-8 SERVINGS

1 cup finely chopped onion

1 large clove garlic

2 teaspoons oil

1 pound ground turkey

1-28 ounce can crushed tomatoes

1 can dark red kidney beans drained and rinsed

¼ teaspoon finely diced jalapeño pepper (wear rubber gloves and do not touch your eyes)

1 cup diced green peppers

1 cup diced carrots

1 diced celery

Seasonings

5 teaspoons brown sugar

5 teaspoons mild chili powder

1 tablespoon ground cumin

1 tablespoon oregano

½ teaspoon coriander

⅛ ground cloves

⅛ teaspoon ground allspice

1. Heat canola oil in a Dutch oven or stockpot. Add onion until translucent. Add the ground turkey, browning it and stirring it to break up pieces. Add the garlic and sauté for an additional 1-2 minutes.

2. Add the tomatoes and all the seasonings. Heat the mixture until it is bubbly. Reduce to simmer with the lid on for about 30 minutes.

3. Add the kidney beans and all vegetables. Continue to simmer until the carrots are softened Chili can be made in advance. I like to serve chili with cornbread/muffins. Jiffy brand is my favorite.

M.Y. Goulash

Most everyone likes Goulash and everyone who makes it has their own version.
Here's mine.

7-8 SERVINGS

What I love about Goulash is that everyone makes their own version. Here is mine. If you don't have a recipe of your own, start with this and make it yours. Maybe you don't like celery in yours. Don't add it. Some don't bake theirs afterwards, as it is not necessary because everything is already cooked before putting it all together. Don't bake yours if you don't have the time. You probably have most everything on hand, or it's easy to keep on hand with ground beef in the freezer. You'll just need to thaw it in the fridge, in cold water, in the sink, or in the refrigerator. This is an easy dish to make for a crowd. This serves 7-8 depending on the serving size. YUM!

2 tablespoons extra virgin olive oil

1 pound ground beef (I like sirloin.)

½ cup chopped white onion

⅓ cup chopped celery

⅓ cup green pepper

⅓ cup orange pepper

⅓ diced carrots

3 cloves garlic

⅓ cup dry red wine

8 ounces dry/uncooked pasta (macaroni or medium shells), cooked as directed and drained

1-28 ounce can crushed tomatoes

1 ½ teaspoons chopped fresh oregano

¼ teaspoon salt

⅛ teaspoon freshly ground black pepper

⅓ cup freshly grated Parmesan cheese and an additional tablespoon to sprinkle over when done if desired

½ cup of mini tomatoes, cut in half

¼ cup chopped fresh parsley

1. Preheat oven to 350 degrees.

2. Heat olive oil in a large Dutch oven. When oil is hot, add ground beef. Stir with a fork to crumble. You want no large clumps. A potato masher works well too.

3. When there is no pink left in the meat, add the chopped onion, stirring occasionally. When the onion becomes translucent (about 6- 7 minutes), add celery, peppers, and carrots. When they are soft (about 5 minutes), add the garlic. Stir for an additional 1-2 minutes. Do not let the garlic burn.

4. Add the red wine, lightly scraping the pan with a wooden spoon to remove the brown bits. Add oregano, salt, and pepper. Continue to stir until wine evaporates.

5. Add the can of crushed tomatoes. Stir to blend all meat and vegetables. Now add the fresh mini tomatoes and stir in the Parmesan cheese. Cook an additional 4-5 minutes. Turn heat off and stir in parsley.

6. Cover and place in the 350-degree preheated oven for 15 minutes.

7. Serve it to bowl or plates with a sprinkle of Parmesan cheese if desired.

Boeuf Bourguignon

Prepared in the slow cooker is the perfect "special occasion company meal" because you can make it ahead. It's an entire entree' in a bowl, and everyone can serve themself. The next day, you have an amazing Encore Meal (leftovers).

6-8 SERVINGS

Every year we take the kids on a ski trip. We skip around between the different ski destinations. Each place has its own flavor, and it is really hard for me to pick a favorite town or place to ski. However, I have a few favorite restaurants from each location. At Snowmass in Colorado, one of our favorite places was a place on the mountain that no longer exists, called Cafe' Suzanne. Cafe Suzanne served the best Boeuf Bourguignon, which is actually a French beef stew.

When we ended up with a foreign exchange student from Perpignan, France, I decided it was a good idea to make our own Boeuf Bourguignon. After reading a few recipes, I came up with a good one on the stove. Then one day I said, "If I can make a beef stew in the slow cooker why can't I make Boeuf Bourguignon as well? Well, I tried, and here is what I came up with. Even though most of the cooking does occur in the slow cooker, you do need to cook the bacon on the stove and brown the beef. This is actually better the next day because the juices meld, giving the stew more flavor. I like to serve it over mashed potatoes, and of the store-bought variety, my favorite is Bob Evans. Yes, you could make them, but the Boeuf Bourguignon is the "Star," and the potatoes are secondary. So why spend the time? It gives you time for a little glass of wine, right?

1 tablespoon extra-virgin olive oil

6 ounces good bacon diced

3 tablespoons unbleached flour (for coating beef)

2 ½ pounds beef chuck, cut into stew pieces

Sea salt

Freshly ground black pepper

¾ pound carrots, peeled and cut into approximately 1-inch diagonal pieces

1 ½ cup yellow onions, thinly sliced

3 teaspoons minced garlic

½ cup Brandy

750 ml bottle good dry red wine

2 cups beef broth (I like Better than Bouillon.)

1 tablespoon tomato paste

1 teaspoon fresh thyme

4 tablespoons unsalted butter (slightly softened and cut into pieces)

3 tablespoons unbleached flour (to dissolve in water to thicken liquid)

1 pound/package frozen pearl onions

1 pound mushrooms trimmed and sliced thick

Fresh parsley

1. Begin by browning the beef. Heat the oil in a skillet, coat the beef in the flour, season with salt and pepper, and sear on all sides. Remove the beef with a slotted spoon or a fork, and place seared beef in the slow cooker.

2. Now cook the bacon with the juices left in the pan.

3. Pour the juices and the bacon in the slow cooker on top of the seared beef.

4. Place all ingredients except the flour and parsley into the slow cooker.

5. Turn on low for 8-10 hours or high for 5-7 hours.

6. About an hour before completed cooking time, mix 3 tablespoons of flour with 3 tablespoons of water in a measuring cup with a fork or mini whisk. Pour into slow cooker and cook for remaining hour.

7. When Boeuf Bourguignon is done, stir in chopped fresh parsley. If desired, serve over mashed potatoes.

Beverages

I make my own lemonade and sweet tea during the warmer months sweetened with agave, a natural sweetener.

6-8 SERVINGS

Lemonade with Agave

½ cup fresh squeezed lemon juice

½ cup light agave syrup

1 quart of cold water

1. Stir together.

2. Serve over lots of ice or store in the refrigerator in a pretty bottle or jug.

Ice Tea Sweetened with Agave

6 decaffeinated tea bags

Pinch of baking soda

¾ cup light agave

2 cups boiling water

6 cups cold water

1. Tie or connect the 6 tea bags to a large clip and place in a large glass measuring cup (or bowl) and steep for 5 minutes.

2. Cover with a plate to keep warm. After the 5 minutes, press/strain tea bags and discard.

3. Add agave and stir.

4. Add 6 cups of water and pour/ladle into a pitcher/glass bottle.

Sangria

One of my favorite summer beverages in the summer is my Sangria.

4 SERVINGS

1 bottle (750 ml) Cruz Garcia Real Sangria in a triangular bottle imported from Spain

½ cup fresh-squeezed orange juice

2 oranges washed. One to slice for sangria and one for garnish.

1. Pour Sangria into a pitcher.

2. Add orange juice and orange slices. Stir.

3. Serve in glasses over lots of ice with an orange slice for garnish on the side of each glass.

Epilogue

When the actual process of writing THIS book began in December of 2019, as a Christmas gift from my dear husband to have an opportunity to realize my dream of writing and publishing a book, little did I realize that the actual process began at age 12 in science class when I decided I did not like studying birds and clouds. In that seventh-grade classroom, I sat there listening to the characteristics of our 'bird of the week' that we were introduced to every Monday, followed by a quiz on Friday over all of the birds we had studied. Our teacher loved birds, and she figured we should too. I DO NOT LIKE BIRDS, never did.

Following the short bird lesson, we began the next unit to be studied, clouds. Really? What is the weatherman for, I thought. I can buy into studying the human body. Birds and clouds ... NOPE. So I tuned out and fortunately, Mrs. Torpe did not notice (her husband actually was a weatherman at the local airport), and my writing career began that day. At that time, I wrote fictional short stories. They were nothing special, and I filled journal after journal, hid them away on a shelf, and went on with my life, doing all of those things one does ... finishing middle school, graduating high school, going on to college, starting a teaching career, getting married, having children, and then a grandchild.

I continued to write over the years here and there, and then in 2017, when the youngest kiddo was settled into his second year of college, I found myself writing Facebook posts about my everyday life. Most everyone began or ended with "It's a Great Day To..." The short posts became longer, describing dinners, parties, lunches with Friends, Family gatherings, trips, workouts, basically the little mundane details, what most people would consider incidental tasks and moments in life. The posts turned into a Home Economics class for kids and adults, volunteering assignments in local elementary schools, Zoom Entertaining classes, then a website, and all of that led to an opportunity to write a book.

So when faced with an opportunity to write a book, someone asked me, "So what will YOU write about?" I thought for a moment and then it came to me, "It's a Great Day To ... Gather Around a Table. Yeah, THAT IS IT!" I started a diagram as Michelle Prince, my book publisher, recommended. It took me a little less than an hour, and the outline was there, as I had been writing it subconsciously in my mind over the years. I just didn't know it until I put the marker to the paper. It was all there back in January of 2020. It just needed to be perfected, edited, photographed, and documented. It should have been easy to pull together with all of the ideas jotted down over the years of raising kids, events recorded in photographs, and Facebook posts displaying my homemaking and cooking skills.

Even with a labor of love, this lifelong dream of a book, the PEOPLE in your life always come first. I would tell my kids as they were growing up, "People are more important than things," and I truly believe that. So when my services, time, or listening ear are needed, my PEOPLE KNOW that they can count on me to be there. So, what I had hoped to be ready for publication on my Birthday, September 9, is a bit delayed, and it's quite all right. There were times during these past seven months when this would cause some frustration, but then one Sunday afternoon in July, as I was typing away and getting frustrated because I was behind on my personal timeline and I realized that I have fewer tech skills than I thought, I sat back and thought to myself, " If you are going to write a book about slowing down and taking the time to Gather Around a Table with the people you love and you have rushed through to write this book, blowing off the people who you cared about along the way, what does that say about you and your credibility on this subject?" It changed my attitude about having fallen behind. We all have choices in our lives and how we live, how we spend our time, and where our hearts are. There were many times when I would have set aside an afternoon or a day to write, and I was needed in one way or another. I made the choice to take the call or help because people ARE more important than things.

I pray for many more meals and memories to make with Stella and the grandchildren and great-grandchildren to follow.

There are times we can do that and times when we can't, and each one of us knows when we can and when we can't. It's only for us to be comfortable with those decisions, and they need not be explained to anyone. We all make the choices that are right for us and our Families, and that is the way it should be.

In these pages, I hope you can see what you already ARE doing that brings the people you care for together. I hope you got some ideas that you can take or alter to make things happen for you in your own special way. Today, there are so many sources for ideas and inspiration that it can all be overwhelming. When you feel like this, follow what your heart says and listen to the voice inside of you. YOU know what your own situation requires and what is realistic for each stage in your own life. DO NOT LET ANYONE INTIMIDATE YOU and make you feel that your way of gathering your people together is not enough. Keep things simple, and focus on the reason for it all. Each time you do it, it will become easier, and you will become more confident.

In closing, I recommend keeping good record of your recipes and what you do. It will help you the next time you go to make the recipe, and it will be something you can share with those you love who ask for that favorite recipe. It can be something as simple as a handwritten journal or notebook, or with the ease of making photo books through an online site or the local pharmacy, it's a great project that can be for you or you and a child as a keepsake for generations to come, with photos to go along with the recipes, of times enjoyed that tell a story. Every day on this earth can be a gift to be enjoyed.

It's a Great Day!